LET'S LEARN TO READ T

Level 1

With Diagrams & Notes for Teachers and Parents!

Dr. Musharraf Hussain Al-Azhari

© **Invitation Publishing**
Sixth Edition 2019

Designed By: Nottingham Printers & Signs

Instructions For Teachers and Parents

"The best amongst you is the one
who learns and then teaches the Quran"
(Bukhari: Reported by Ali ﷺ)

The Majestic Quran is the speech of Allah Almighty; these are divine words revealed to the la
messenger Muhammad ﷺ in clear and beautiful Arabic. The Quranic verses are melodious a
rhythmic yet they are not poetry. Muslims must learn to read the divine revelation in its origin
Arabic language . Parents in the past as well as today throughout the Muslim world were, and a
eager to teach their five and six year old children to read the Quran.

The benefits and merits of reading the Quran are enormous; the Prophet ﷺ said there are te
merits for reading each letter of the Quran and alif-lamm-meem are three letters, their reward is thi
merits. On another occasion he said "a person who doesn't know anything from the Quran is like
derelict house" (Tirmizi).

This manual has been written for beginners, it will be useful for all age's even children as young
five or six will be able to use it (Insha-Allah). With guidance from teachers and parents the
principles of Quran reading can be mastered in a short period of time.

It is important for the English speaking learner to familiarise themselves with the Arabic script so th
they can pronounce the syllables and then make words without having to look at the transliteratio
The transliteration should be used to counter check doubts in pronunciation. If the rules of readir
are properly learnt and thoroughly practiced by doing all the exercise then the pupil will begin to rea
the Holy Quran very quickly.

Throughout this manual the focus has been on developing both the phonological awareness and th
mental resource bank of known words. Although some children will prefer one than the other
learning to read, nevertheless both methods are useful. By taking this structured approach in bo
methods children will learn quickly.

Acknowledgment:
This manual is based on three very famous manuals;
Yassarn-Al-Quran by Qari Muhammad Ismael
Noorani Qaida by Qari Noor Muhammad
Ahsan-ul-Qawaid by Qari Shamsuddin Barudwi
May Allah bless the soul of these teachers of the glorious Quran.

I would like to thank all those who helped me to complete this task in particular I am grateful to An
Iftikhar, Zahid Mahmood, Abdulrahman & Dr. Amjad Aziz.

Dr. Musharraf Hussain
Nottingham

September 2019

 بسم الله	ب	 الله	ا
 ثمر	ث	 تاج	ت
 حج	ح	 جنّت	ج
 دار	د	 خبز	خ

ذ

ذئب

ر

رمضان

ز

زهرة

س

سلام عليكم

ش

شمس

ص

صلاة

ض

ضان

ط

طفل

	ع
	عين

	ظ
	ظرف

	ف
	فلک

	غ
	غنم

	ك
	كتاب

	ق
	قرآن

	م
	محمّد

	ل
	لااله الاالله

 ن

نجم

 و

وضوء

 ع

أرض

 ة ﺓ

هرّة

 ي

يد

he 29 Letters of the Arabic alphabet must be memorised. Their correct
ronunciation and shapes must be learnt. They should be learnt in their
roups i.e. letters with similar shapes. Remember that Arabic starts from
e right hand side.

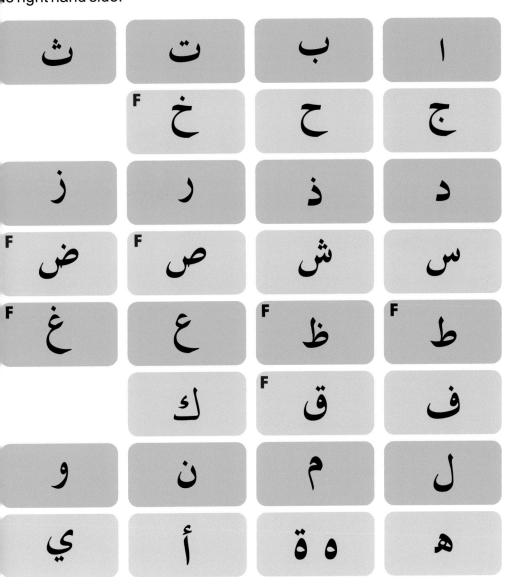

ث	ت	ب	ا
خ **F**	ح		ج
ز	ر	ذ	د
ض **F**	ص **F**	ش	س
غ **F**	ع	ظ **F**	ط **F**
	ك	ق **F**	ف
و	ن	م	ل
ي	أ	ة ه	ه

F: These 7 letters are pronounced with full mouth.

5

Please read the following letters very carefully. Pronounce them so you can tell a difference between them.

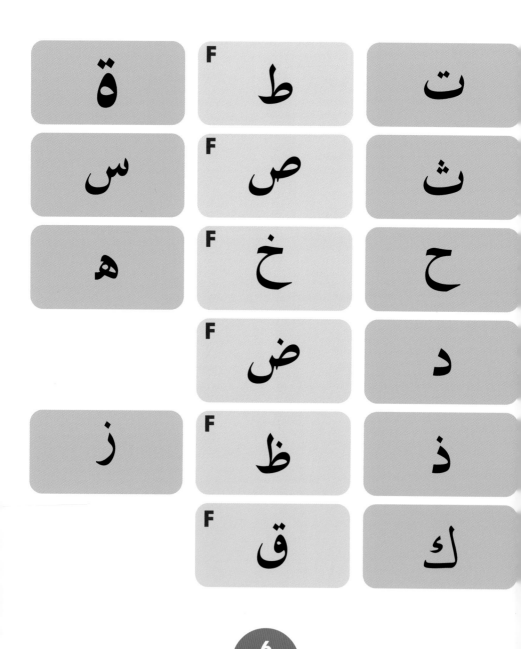

ت	ط F	ق
ث	ص F	س
ح	خ F	ه
د	ض F	
ذ	ظ F	ز
ك	ق F	

hese are randomly organised letters, test yourself. Can you recognise the
ndividual letters?

ط	س	د	ج	ب
ر	م	ن	ث	ا
ظ	ع	ح	ش	ذ
ق	ض	ص	ز	ت
ف	خ	ق	ى	غ
ز	ء	خ	ث	ه
و	ت	ل	ك	ط
ع	ة	س	ز	ذ

EXERCISE 2 LETTER RECOGNITION EXERCISE

The apples have a letter written on them, read them out starting from (start here!) and follow the arrows.

EXERCISE 3 LETTER RECOGNITION EXERCISE

Each balloon has a letter written on it, read it out and then tie it to the brick with the same letter written on it.

FULL LETTER

ت

MIDDLE   **BEGINNING**

ـتـ   تـ

END

ـت

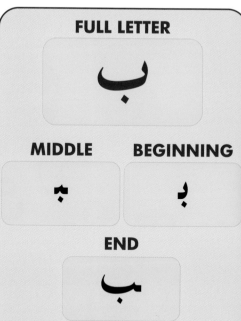

FULL LETTER

ب

MIDDLE   **BEGINNING**

ـبـ   بـ

END

ـب

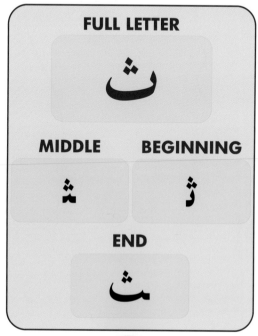

FULL LETTER

ث

MIDDLE   **BEGINNING**

ـثـ   ثـ

END

ـث

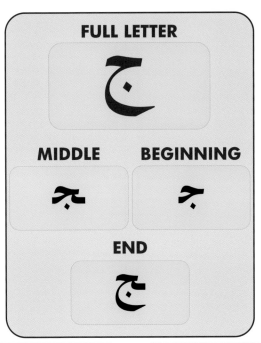

FULL LETTER

ج

MIDDLE   BEGINNING

END

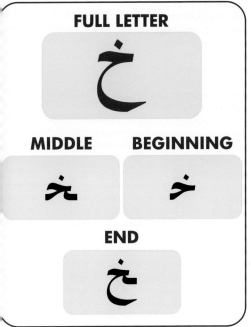

FULL LETTER

خ

MIDDLE   BEGINNING

END

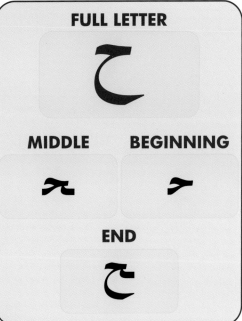

FULL LETTER

ح

MIDDLE   BEGINNING

END

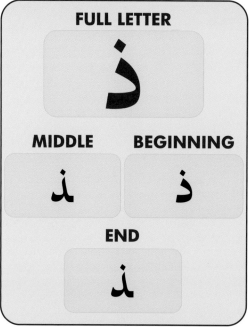

FULL LETTER

ذ

MIDDLE   **BEGINNING**

ـذ   ذ

END

ـذ

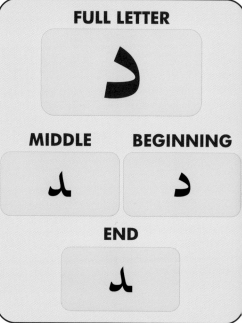

FULL LETTER

د

MIDDLE   **BEGINNING**

ـد   د

END

ـد

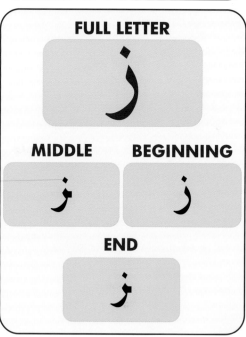

FULL LETTER

ز

MIDDLE   **BEGINNING**

ـز   ز

END

ـز

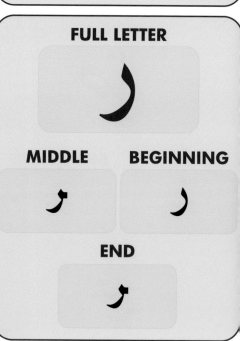

FULL LETTER

ر

MIDDLE   **BEGINNING**

ـر   ر

END

ـر

FULL LETTER

ش

MIDDLE ـشـ **BEGINNING** شـ

END ـش

FULL LETTER

س

MIDDLE ـسـ **BEGINNING** سـ

END ـس

FULL LETTER

ض

MIDDLE ـضـ **BEGINNING** ضـ

END ـض

FULL LETTER

ص

MIDDLE ـصـ **BEGINNING** صـ

END ـص

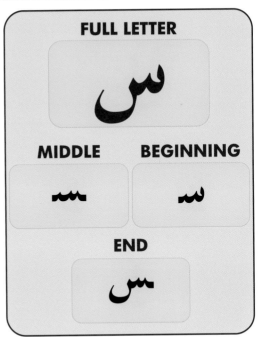

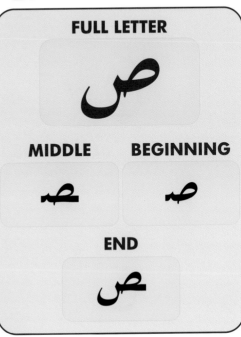

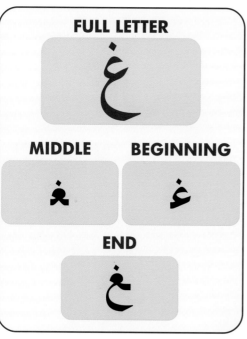

FULL LETTER
ق

MIDDLE
ﻘ

BEGINNING
ﻗ

END
ﻖ

FULL LETTER
ف

MIDDLE
ﻔ

BEGINNING
ﻓ

END
ﻒ

FULL LETTER
ك

MIDDLE
ﻜ

BEGINNING
ﻛ

END
ﻚ

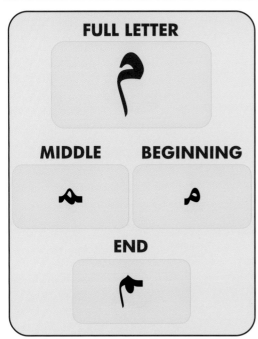

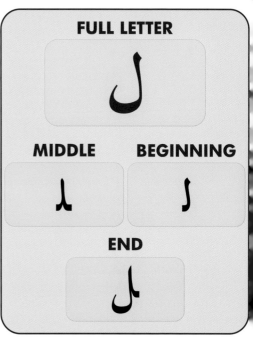

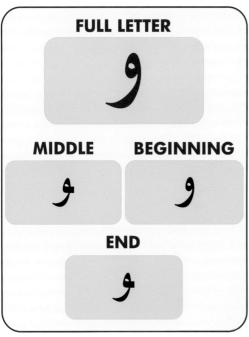

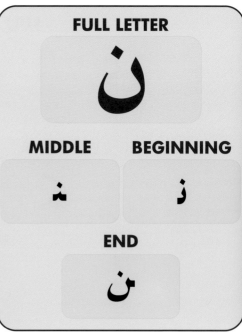

FULL LETTER

ق

END

ـة ة

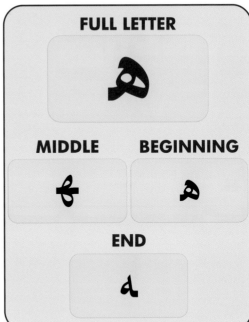

FULL LETTER

ه

MIDDLE

ـهـ

BEGINNING

هـ

END

ـه

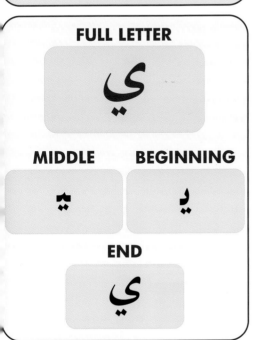

FULL LETTER

ي

MIDDLE

ـيـ

BEGINNING

يـ

END

ـي

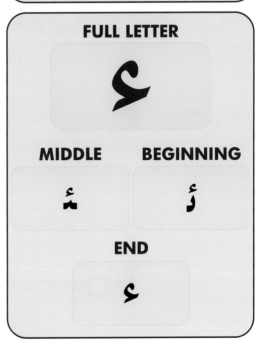

FULL LETTER

ء

MIDDLE

ـئـ

BEGINNING

أ

END

ء

Which letters have got on the bus?
Read them out aloud.

Read the letters inside the flowers.

بلغ	أمر
ذكر	رفع
ظلم	صدق
حكم	وزر
مثل	خلق

حسد	جمع
سرق	زعم
خسف	ضرب
ظهر	وهب
صحف	سئل

ذرأ	مرج
نظر	كفر
حضر	غفر
فتح	نبذ
وهو	أذن

22

رفث	عبس
فعل	فرض
ترك	هلك
جعل	أخذ
حشر	تضع

خلق	ذهب
كتب	صرف
ورق	سخر
ملك	بقى
قدر	يهب

علم	أرم
شية	برق
خسر	شيع
يلج	حبط
لعن	يضع

شرب	يئس
غضب	أثر
عوج	شهد
كره	حسب
وضع	كثر

26

تبع	عمل
ترن	سفه
نبا	رحم
فلم	رضى
زبر	جعل

خطف	قبل
وسع	فرح
غسق	سخط
يدى	تجد
خبث	يرث

خلق	هدى
كبر	قرى
منع	يعد
تزر	كتب
أخر	رسل

MISSION STATEMENT

To help individuals and families learn life skills, develop moral and spiritual values through education, worship and recreation.

EDUCATION

COMMUNITY

DAWAH

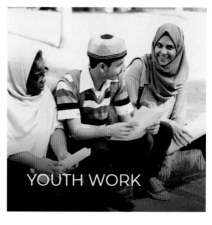

YOUTH WORK

www.karimia.com